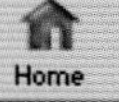

Come on a Des

written by Rachel Sparks Linfield

Contents

Back Forward Stop Refresh Home Print

Favorites History Search Scrapbook Page Holder

Come on a Desert Safari!

Many people think that deserts are just hot, dry, sandy places. They think that no one can live in a desert. They think that no plants can grow and that no animals can survive. *These people are wrong!*

- Some deserts are very hot in the daytime but become freezing cold at night.
- Rain does fall sometimes.

☼ Not all deserts are sandy.

A stony desert

A sandy desert

Deserts are *amazing*, so choose your destination and book your holiday with us, the Desert Safari specialists!

Back  Forward Stop  Refresh  Home  Print

Favorites History Search Scrapbook Page Holder

Choose your desert!

Each desert is different. To choose the desert for your safari you must think carefully about what you would like to see …
Exciting scenery?
Prickly plants?
Rare animals?

Death Valley

Sonora

Desert Safari Travel rating symbols

 Very hot sun

 Interesting landscape

 Cacti

 Trees

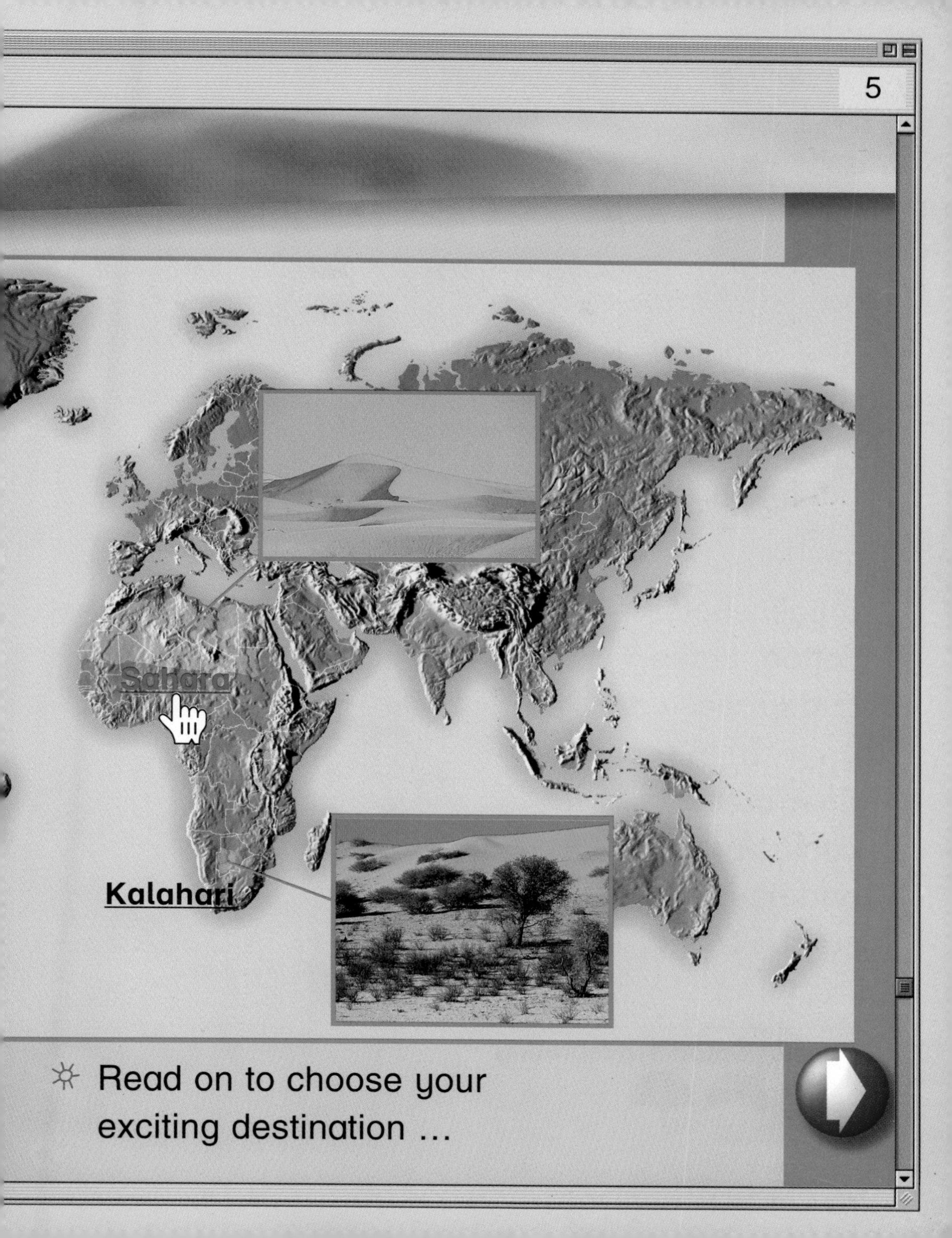

Read on to choose your exciting destination ...

For amazing sand, visit the Sahara!

The Sahara is the largest desert in the world. It can be extremely hot in the summer.

One fifth of the Sahara is made up of ***sand dunes****.*

There are damp areas where cotton, dates and grapes can grow. In the drier areas cactus plants and desert rats can be found.

Desert Safari Travel rating

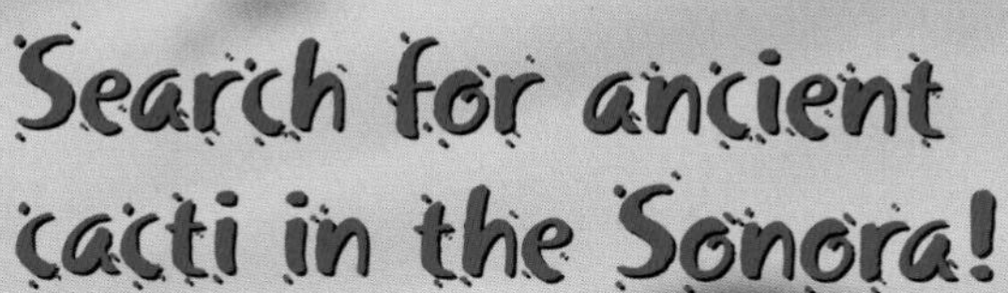

Search for ancient cacti in the Sonora!

If you love cacti, you must visit **this** desert. It has over 300 varieties!

Desert Safari Travel rating

Stop

Print

Favorites History Search Scrapbook Page Holder

See Death Valley's amazing "golf course!"

Death Valley is a rocky desert. It is the hottest, driest place in North America.

In one part of the valley there used to be a lake … about 2000 years ago. When the lake **evaporated** it left a thick layer of salt. This area is known as the Devil's Golf Course.

Desert Safari Travel rating

WARNING Travellers must be well prepared for extremely dry, hot conditions.

For terrific trees, go on safari in the Kalahari!

The Kalahari Desert is a hot desert with dry riverbeds running across it. It is famous for its *enormous* baobab trees.

Some of the trees are 2000 years old and have hollow trunks that measure up to 20 metres around.

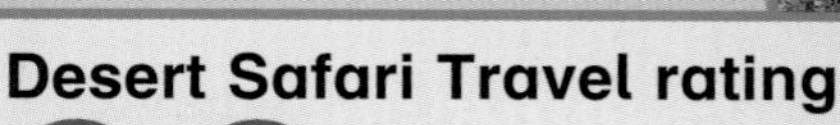

Desert Safari Travel rating

A huge baobab tree

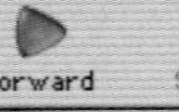

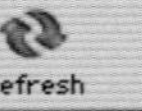

Experience a different way of life!

Desert people survive because they know their surroundings well. They know:

- how to find water and use it sensibly
- where to look for food
- how to protect themselves from strong winds and sun

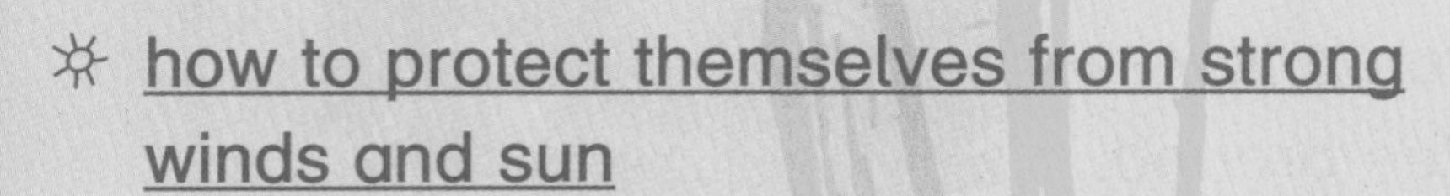

- how to travel great distances safely
- which animals could harm them.

You too could know all this if you visit a desert!

Finding water

You can survive the heat of the desert if you know where the water is.

Water can often be found in an **oasis**.

Some desert people live in one place. Others are **nomads** who move from place to place searching for water and **fertile land**.

Learn to find water with reeds!

In the Kalahari Desert, water is very precious, as it is in all deserts. The San people can use hollow reeds as straws to suck water out of the ground.

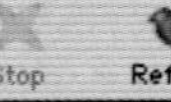

Learn to live in a tent – and travel by camel

The Tuareg people are nomads who live in the Sahara. They live in tents made of goat hair. Many Tuareg people travel on camels with herds of sheep and goats. Some use motorbikes instead of camels.

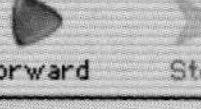

See the deserts bloom!

A desert may look dry and dead, but when the rain does come, it turns into a carpet of flowers. The flowers bloom for a short time, produce seed, and then die. So if you want to see desert flowers, make sure you visit at the right time.

WARNING Please note that Desert Safari Travel cannot guarantee rain during your safari.

See the deserts bloom!

Desert plants must be able to store the precious rain water until it rains again. Different plants do this in lots of different ways.

Cacti

Sonora Page 7

Many cacti grow in the deserts of America. Saguaro cacti can be as tall as 15 metres and can live for 200 years!

Fleshy, thick stems store water.

Roots spread out underground to find as much water as possible.

Euphorbia trees

Euphorbia trees store water as juice.

Prickly spines stop animals from eating the trees.

Acacia trees

Extremely long roots search for water.

Meet the weird and wonderful animals!

Over the years, desert animals have had to change to fit their tough surroundings.

In a desert you can learn how animals:

- save water
- protect themselves from heat
- scare enemies
- walk on sand.

If you are lucky you might see one of these:

Darkling beetles

Death Valley Page 8

Darkling beetles can live for more than four months without eating.

Air between the body and wing covers protects beetles from desert heat.

Rattlesnakes

This snake rattles loose rings of skin on its tail to scare enemies. Snakes in other parts of the world hiss at their enemies, but hissing uses water, so desert snakes don't hiss.

Desert lizards

Scaly skin helps to save water.

Front legs can be pushed hard to lift head and body high above very hot desert sand.

WARNING You will have to search for some of the animals at night. They may be dangerous. Do not approach them without your expert Desert Safari Travel guide.

Favorites History Search Scrapbook Page Holder

Fennec foxes

Fennec foxes do not drink. They get liquid from the plants and animals they eat.

Large ears help with cooling. Blood is cooled by air blowing across the ears. The blood then keeps the body cool as it flows around the body.

Desert spiders

A thin layer of wax stops water evaporating from the body.

Geckoes

Webbed feet with hairy fringes prevent this lizard sinking into the sand.

Rent-a-camel

Top quality camels! The best way to travel in the desert!

Every camel has:

- *a hump to store fat*
- *two webbed toes on each foot to stop it sinking in sand*
- *nostrils that close in sandstorms*
- *long eyelashes to keep sand out of its eyes.*

Every camel can:

- survive without food or water for up to ten days!

So, book your camel now! Satisfaction guaranteed!

Come on a Desert Safari now!

If you have a taste for excitement and want to know more about the planet you live on, then book your holiday now. You will not be disappointed!

See desert flowers

Meet desert people

Explore the desert landscape

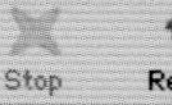

Print

Favorites History Search Scrapbook Page Holder

Booking form

Name of desert traveller:

Address:

Reasons for wanting to visit a desert:

Questions about the desert you would like to answer on your safari:

Desert choice:

Sahara → page 6

Sonora → page 7

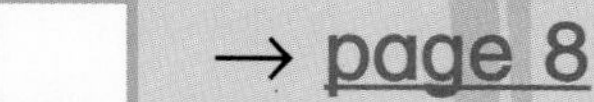

Death Valley → page 8

Kalahari → page 9

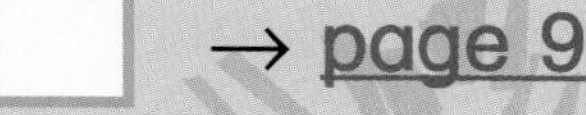

Messages from desert travellers

"The sand dunes in the Sahara were amazing. Now I'm trying to make some in my sand pit."
Misha, Edinburgh

"I found 98 sorts of cactus in the Sonoran Desert. They were really pretty but they had huge prickles. Ouch!"
Poppy, Bristol

"The Devil's Golf Course was fantastic. I couldn't believe it was made of salt. I took hundreds of photos." Derrick, Birmingham

Glossary

absorb	take in
evaporated	dried up
fertile land	ground in which plants grow well
nomads	people with no fixed home who move from place to place
oasis	place in a desert where water can be found
sand dunes	hills of sand made by winds

Back Forward Stop Refresh Home Print

Favorites History Search Scrapbook Page Holder

Index